WESTBURY TO TAUNTON

Vic Mitchell and Keith Smith

MP Middleton Press

Published January 2002

ISBN 1 901706 76 1

© Middleton Press, 2002

Design   David Pede
Typesetting   Barbara Mitchell

Published by
            Middleton Press
            Easebourne Lane
            Midhurst, West Sussex
            GU29 9AZ
Tel: 01730 813169
Fax: 01730 812601

Printed & bound by Biddles Ltd,
            Guildford and Kings Lynn

CONTENTS

ACKNOWLEDGEMENTS

We are very grateful for the help received from many of the photographers mentioned in the credits and also for the assistance received from R.M.Casserley, G.Croughton, M.King, N.Langridge, Mr D. & Dr S.Salter, R.Sims, C.P.Stacey, E.Youldon; and we make special mention of our ever helpful wives, Barbara Mitchell and Janet Smith, as this book was compiled during the period in which we celebrated the 20th anniversary of our first volume. Their backing is greatly appreciated.

I. The 1947 Railway Clearing House map shows GWR routes with hollow lines.

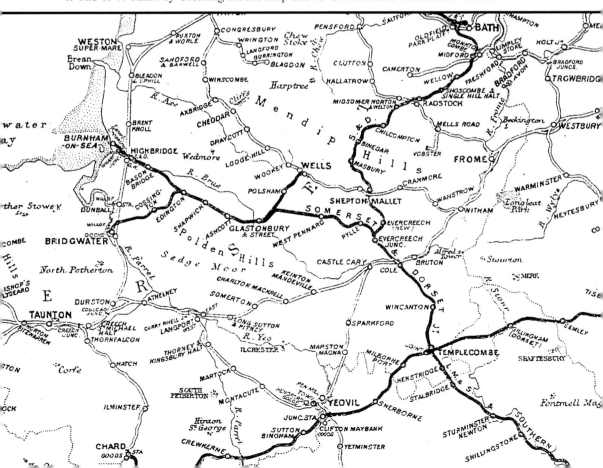

GEOGRAPHICAL SETTING

The route starts at the former iron producing country town of Westbury, which is situated on a narrow outcrop of Upper Greensand containing that metal. The first two miles are in Wiltshire, the remaining being in Somerset.

The line climbs over Corallian Limestone to enter the valley of the River Frome at Frome, another but larger town of great antiquity and local importance. Its fortune was based on wool. The tracks follow this narrowing river as far as Witham and continue over Limestones which form a southern extension of the Cotswolds. The River Brue passes through a gap in this ridge and the railway follows this west-flowing watercourse as far as Keinton Mandeville. There is an almost continuous down gradient for 12 miles.

The 1906 route from Castle Cary is on much gentler gradients than the old line to Weymouth and traverses mainly Lower Lias clay to Somerton, a small town with an ancient market cross. Marl is reached near Langport, which was once an inland port for coastal shipping. Thereafter, the line crosses moors and marshland adjacent to the Rivers Parrett and Tone to reach the historic county town of Somerset, Taunton.

The maps are to the scale of 25ins to 1 mile, unless otherwise stated.

HISTORICAL BACKGROUND

The Bristol & Exeter Railway reached Taunton on 1st July 1842 and was extended to Exeter on 1st May 1844.

The Wilts, Somerset & Weymouth Railway branched from the London - Bath line at Thingley Junction and was opened to Westbury on 5th September 1848. It was extended to Frome on 7th October 1850, to Radstock on 15th November 1854 and to Yeovil (Pen Mill) on 1st September 1856. The Salisbury to Warminster line was completed on 30th June 1856 and a branch from Witham to Shepton Mallet followed on 9th November 1858.

The BER opened a branch from Durston to Yeovil (Hendford) on 1st October 1853. All the above lines were built to the broad gauge of 7ft 0¼ins. The Great Western Railway absorbed the WSWR in 1850 and the BER in 1876. A third rail for standard gauge trains was added thus: Durston to Langport in 1867 and Durston to Taunton in 1875. The Westbury - Castle Cary section was narrowed in June 1874.

To avoid trains between London and Weymouth having to travel via Devizes, a line from Patton & Chirton to Westbury was provided in 1900. A link between the Weymouth line at Castle Cary and the Exeter line at Cogload Junction (south of Durston) was opened for through goods traffic on 11th June 1906 and for passengers on 2nd July 1906. Parts of it were

II. The 4 miles to 1 inch map of 1946 reveals the location of some the intermediate stations and halts.

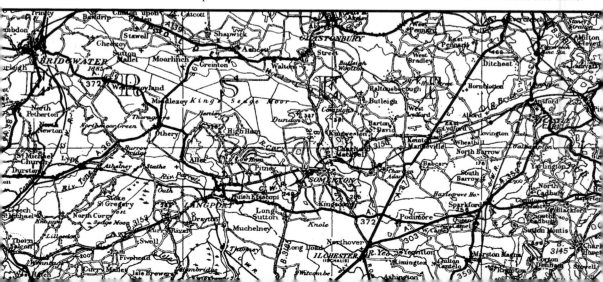

brought into use earlier: Castle Cary to Charlton Mackrell for passengers and goods on 1st July 1905, to Somerton for goods from the west on 12th February 1906 and the section bypassing Durston was used by goods trains from 2nd April 1906. The new route cut 20 miles off the journey between London and the West. Further bypasses (or cut-offs in GWR parlance) were provided: at Westbury (on 1st January 1933) and at Frome (on the next day), these further speeding expresses to the West. Both are still in use.

The lines became part of the Western Region of British Railways upon nationalisation in 1948. Subsequent station closures are detailed in the captions. Privatisation changes in the mid-1990s eventually resulted in most through trains on the route being worked by First Great Western and Weymouth services by Wales & West. The latter became Wessex Trains in this area on 14th October 2001.

III. Gradient profile.

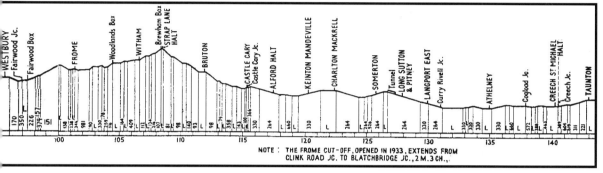

NOTE : THE FROME CUT-OFF, OPENED IN 1933, EXTENDS FROM CLINK ROAD JC. TO BLATCHBRIDGE JC., 2 M. 3 CH.,

PASSENGER SERVICES

Only down stopping trains running at least five days per week are considered in this section.

Weymouth trains provided five weekday and two Sunday services between Westbury and Castle Cary in most years to 1906. An example of the initial limited timetable on part of the new route is shown below. The following summary indicates the train frequency east and west of Castle Cary in selected years.

	Westbury - Castle Cary		Castle Cary - Taunton	
	Weekdays	*Sundays*	*Weekdays*	*Sundays*
1908	7	3	4	1
1928	7	2	6	1
1948	8	5	5	1
1962	7	0	3	0

Local traffic on the new section west of Castle Cary was always worked as if the route was a branch off the London-Weymouth main line. Thus most services commenced at Castle Cary, although one weekday journey ran to and from Frome into the 1950s. All stopping trains on the western section started at Castle Cary in the final years of the service, some running via Yeovil and calling at Langport West instead of East.

Subsequent to September 1962, Bruton and Frome have been the only intermediate stations (although Witham lasted until 1966) and they have been served by Weymouth trains - in recent times 8 or 9 on weekdays, with 3 or more on Sundays.

IV. October 1905

		mrn	mrn	aft	aft	aft										mrn	aft	aft	aft	aft		
Castle Cary............dep.		9 18	1125	1 18	3 43	6 20							Charlton Mackrell......dep.		9 40	1245	2 10	4 40	6 45		
Keinton Mandeville..........		9 30	1137	1 30	3 55	6 32							Keinton Mandeville		9 46	1251	2 16	4 46	6 51		
Charlton Mackrell.....arr.		9 35	1142	1 35	4 0	6 37							Castle Cary 20; 22.....arr.		9 57	1 2	2 27	4 57	7 2		

"Halt" at Alford.

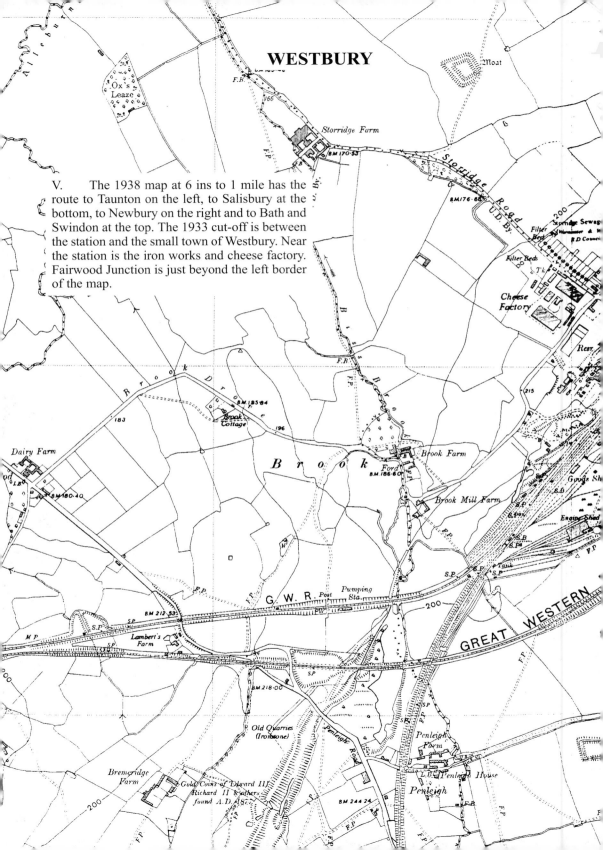

WESTBURY

Moat

Ox's
Leaze

F.B.

166

Storridge Farm

BM 170·53

Storridge Road U.D.Br

BM 176·86

200

Storridge Sewage
Filter Works & M
R D Council
Beds

Filter Beds

Tk

V.   The 1938 map at 6 ins to 1 mile has the
route to Taunton on the left, to Salisbury at the
bottom, to Newbury on the right and to Bath and
Swindon at the top. The 1933 cut-off is between
the station and the small town of Westbury. Near
the station is the iron works and cheese factory.
Fairwood Junction is just beyond the left border
of the map.

Cheese
Factory

Rest.

F.B.

215

Brook

Brook
Dairy Farm
L.B.

BM 195·84

BM 180·40

183

Brook
Cottage

196

B r o o k

Ford
BM 186·60

Brook Farm

Goods Sh

S.B.

S.Po

Brook Mill Farm

Engine Shed

S.Po

S.B.

S.P.

W

S.P.
S.P. Tank
S.P.

Pumping
Sta.
F.P.

G. W. R.   Post
PW
200

BM 212·53

S.P.

Lambert's
Farm

S.P.

GREAT WESTERN

M P

S.P.

BM 218·00

S.P.

S.P.

FP

Old Quarries
(Ironstone)

Penleigh Road

Penleigh
Farm

L.B. Penleigh House

Bremeridge
Farm

Gold Coins of Edward III,
Richard II & others
found A.D. 1807

BM 244·24

F.B.

Penleigh

200

1.   The direct route from Newbury was opened in 1900 and the station was enlarged to four platforms in readiness for its revised junction status. This southward postcard view includes North Box and an up local goods train, but not the booking office. This is at a low level on the left and is linked to the platforms by a subway. The first station had a footbridge and a roof over both tracks. The staff levels increased from 45 in 1903 to 130 in 1923, partly due to the opening of an engine shed in 1915. (Lens of Sutton)

2.   No. 5937 *Stanford Hall* stands at platform 1 on 15th June 1953, just clear of the often-busy barrow crossing. Much luggage and many parcels changed trains here, as services from five different routes called. (R.S.Carpenter)

3.   Middle Box was situated at the south end of platforms 1-2 and was in use until 5th May 1968. On 9th May 1964, a non-stop run from Paddington to Plymouth was planned to commemorate the 102mph record by *City of Truro* 60 years earlier. However, some firebars melted on no.4079 *Pendennis Castle* and it was taken off the train here. No. 6999 *Capel Dewi Hall* is seen taking its place at short notice. It was mass trespass that brought a total ban on steam for many years. (M.A.N.Johnston)

4.   Recorded south of the station on 1st December 1967 were no. 6998 *Burton Agnes Hall* and 0-4-2T no. 1466 bound for retirement at the Didcot Railway Centre. They had been at Totnes Quay - see pictures 32 and 33 in *Newton Abbot to Plymouth*. (R.E.Toop)

5.   North Box took over the functions of Middle Box in 1968 and also those of South Box on 16th September 1978. No. D1043 departs with an up train bound for Paddington on 17th September 1975, while no. 47505 waits at platform 3 with the 16.20 Weymouth to Cardiff. (T.Heavyside)

6.   No. D1067 was recorded on the same day on the up goods loop with a Yeoman stone train. The track was officially "Up Reception". The yard of 17 sidings to the south had become the centre for Mendip limestone distribution. (T.Heavyside)

Other views of this location can be seen in
Newbury to Westbury, Salisbury to Westbury
and *Westbury to Bath.*

7.   During the total closure of the station from 7th April to 13th May 1984 there were extensive track alterations, which included closure of platform 1. The tall building in the distance housed a new signalling centre for the district thereafter. No. 150221 enters the new platform 1 on 24th November 1994, working the 14.33 Bristol Temple Meads to Weymouth service. (M.J.Stretton)

8.   Seen on the same day at platform 3 is no. 43181 *Devonport Royal Dockyard 1693-1993*. Stone wagons stand nearby; this traffic grew greatly due to increased road building in the South in particular. Local general freight traffic had ceased on 1st November 1966. (M.J.Stretton)

WESTBURY DEPOT

9.　　The location of the steam depot can be found on the map, south of the station. It was opened in April 1915 and part of its massive water tank was photographed on 23rd May 1929, along with no. 218. (H.C.Casserley)

10.   Below the tank was the coal stage, on which small iron tubs were pushed to the doorway seen above the tender of no. 9319 on 14th September 1936. There is a hinged platform which was lowered over the tender and onto which the tub was wheeled for tipping. (H.C.Casserley)

11.   This undated view is soon after the advent of British Railways. At least two engines are clean. Near full employment meant that it was difficult to obtain labour for coaling, ash removal and cleaning. (Wessex coll.)

12.   Heaps of clinker gather on 26th April 1959, as two empty coal wagons stand on the incline to the coal stage. No. 8744 stands out of use with companion pannier tanks. The shed closed in September 1965; it had four parallel roads. (P.J.Kelley)

13.   A diesel fuelling and minor maintenance depot opened in April 1959 and serviced a wide variety of traction types until closure in 1993. No. 46007 waits in the foreground with class 52 no. D1053 *Western Patriarch* behind. To the right of it, a class 31 is being fuelled under the shelter on 16th October 1966. (G.Gillham)

14.   A class 47 and two members of the class 56 were in the diesel sidings on 30th April 1988 and are seen through a telephoto lens from platform 3. The site was remote from the former steam depot, on the opposite side of the running lines. (M.Turvey)

15.   Introduced in 1989, the class 60's Mirlees engines generated 3100hp. No. 60008 was recorded on 24th February 1991. The quarry operators had purchased their own fleets of class 59 diesels in 1985-90. Each had General Motors power units of 3300hp and servicing was undertaken at Merehead Quarry. (M.J.Stretton)

WEST OF WESTBURY

16.　　Class 52 no. D1056 *Western Sultan* approaches Westbury from the south with the 10.05 Weymouth to Bristol on 16th October 1976. When this area was remodelled and resignalled in September 1978, a new chord line was installed across the area in the foreground to allow stone trains from Merehead or Whatley Quarries direct access to the down yard. Wagons stand in the up yard in the background. (G.Gillham)

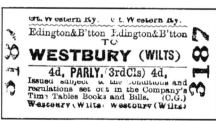

17.   With the White Horse clearly visible in the background, no. 50006 *Neptune* heads the 17.47 Fridays-only Paddington to Plymouth away from Westbury towards Fairwood Junction on 6th July 1984. When illuminated, the feather lights allow access to the down yard via the crossover near the bridge and diamond crossings over the Salisbury lines. (G.Gillham)

18.   The same bridge and the White Horse are visible again as "Britannia" class 4-6-2 no. 70019 *Lightning* speeds westbound on the cut-off on 2nd July 1955. It is about to join the original route (left) at Fairwood Junction. (R.E.Toop)

19.   The previous picture was taken from the roadway on the right. No. 7924 *Thornycroft Hall* is working a Paddington to Weymouth train that has run via Westbury on 23rd April 1955. The 28-lever Fairwood Junction signal box was in use from 1st January 1933 until 11th May 1984. (R.E.Toop)

BRITISH RLYS. (W)   BRITISH RLYS. (W)
FROME   FROME
TO
PADDINGTON
Via Lavington & Theale or Melksham
FIRST CLASS
22/5 H Fare 22/5 H
Paddington   Paddington
FOR CONDITIONS   R CONDITIONS
SEE BACK   SEE BACK

20.   From the bridge in the previous picture, we witness a chance meeting of two ex-works locomotives with stone trains at Fairwood Junction on 12th September 1978. In the foreground no. 46026 *Leicestershire & Derbyshire Yeomanry* heads for Merehead with empty Amey Roadstone hoppers while no. 33205 approaches with a Somerset Quarry to Woking ballast train. (G.Gillham)

21.   No. 6935 *Browsholme Hall* picks up water at speed from Fairwood troughs on 16th July 1955, while working a London to Weymouth service. The supply tank is on the right. There was a signal box at Fairwood level crossing from 1st July 1900 until 1st January 1933. (R.E.Toop)

EAST OF FROME

22.   A little over three miles from Fairwood Junction is Clink Road Junction. No. 5508 is working milk empties from Westbury to Yeovil and is turning off the main line to take the loop to Frome on 29th August 1954. (D.Trevor Rowe)

23.   Hymek class 35 no. D7039 passes the recently repainted signal box at Clink Road Junction with ballast hoppers from Somerset Quarry on 26th March 1970. The junction was remodelled in May 1977, when a single facing crossover replaced the moving-frog diamond crossing seen here. The signal box closed on 6th October 1984, having come into use with the Frome cut-off on 2nd January 1933. (G.Gillham)

24.   The revised layout is evident as a Westbury to Weymouth DMU takes the single line towards Frome on 20th July 1984. The architect had made good provision for signalmen with BO or hallitosis. The frame had 29 levers and was in use until 7th October 1984. (D.H.Mitchell)

25.   No. 33032 was hauling the 06.55 Yeovil Pen Mill to Cardiff on 24th March 1987 when it collided near Frome North Junction with no. 47202 taking empties to Whatley Quarry. It was the driver of the latter that had passed a signal at danger; he was in hospital for a long period. (S.P.McMullin)

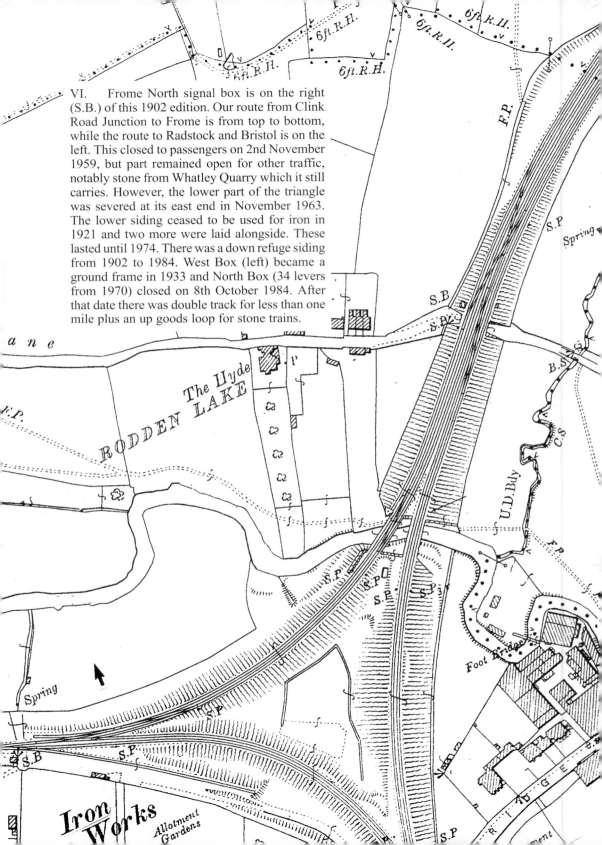

VI. Frome North signal box is on the right (S.B.) of this 1902 edition. Our route from Clink Road Junction to Frome is from top to bottom, while the route to Radstock and Bristol is on the left. This closed to passengers on 2nd November 1959, but part remained open for other traffic, notably stone from Whatley Quarry which it still carries. However, the lower part of the triangle was severed at its east end in November 1963. The lower siding ceased to be used for iron in 1921 and two more were laid alongside. These lasted until 1974. There was a down refuge siding from 1902 to 1984. West Box (left) became a ground frame in 1933 and North Box (34 levers from 1970) closed on 8th October 1984. After that date there was double track for less than one mile plus an up goods loop for stone trains.

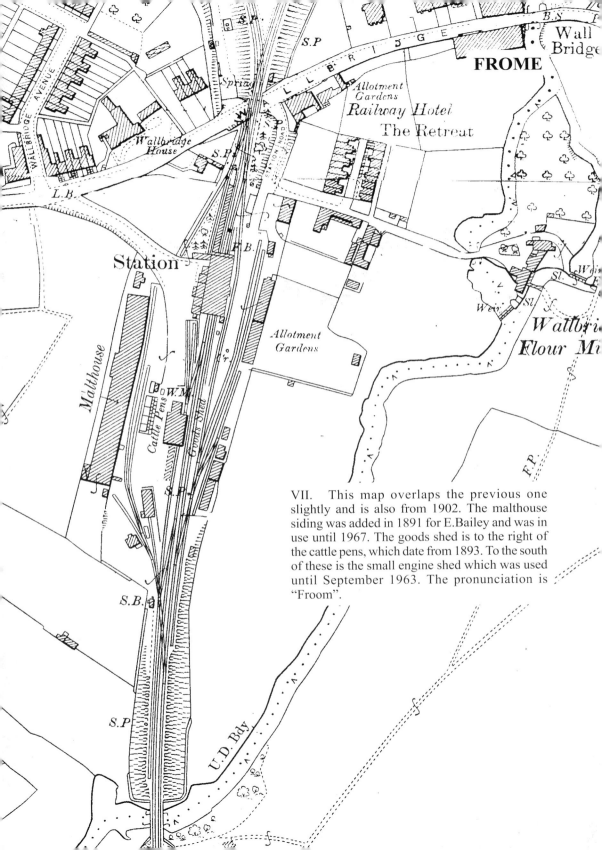

FROME

Wall
Bridge

B.S.

S.P

Allotment Gardens

Railway Hotel

The Retreat

Springs

Wallbridge House

S.P.

L.B.

Station

F.B.

Allotment Gardens

Weir

Sl.

Weir

Sl.

Wallbri
Flour Mi

Malthouse

W.M.

Cattle Pens

Goods Shed

S.P.

VII.   This map overlaps the previous one slightly and is also from 1902. The malthouse siding was added in 1891 for E.Bailey and was in use until 1967. The goods shed is to the right of the cattle pens, which date from 1893. To the south of these is the small engine shed which was used until September 1963. The pronunciation is "Froom".

S.B.

F.P.

S.P

U.D. Bdy

26.   The main building (left) was of timber, whereas other nearby stations with train sheds, such as Cheddar, were stone built. The diagonal structure at the far end of the shed in this 1922 view is part of the external footbridge, which also appears in the next two pictures. It was built in 1875. (LCGB/NRM)

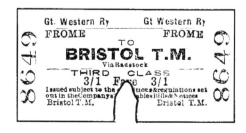

8649

Gt. Western Ry   Gt Western Ry
FROME   FROME
              TO
BRISTOL T.M.
              Via Radstock
    THIRD   CLASS
        3/1   Fare 3/1
Issued subject to the   tions & regulations set
out in the Companys'   ables Bills & Notices
    Bristol T.M.   Bristol T.M.

8649

27.   A snap from a train arriving from Radstock on 24th October 1959 includes South Box which functioned from 17th September 1933 until 19th August 1970, its frame having been reduced from 73 to 28 levers by that time. It replaced an 1875 structure known as "Middle Box". (M.A.N.Johnston)

28.   Coaches stand on the down goods loop and obscure the down goods yard, while passengers wait for a down train. Goods traffic ceased in 1967 at both yards. There was a staff of 42 to 52 in the first 40 years of that century. In the previous century the figures were 5 in 1850, 8 in 1872 and 31 in 1881. (Lens of Sutton)

29.   For two weeks in September 1978, major track alterations at Westbury Station meant that west of England trains due to stop there were diverted to call at Frome instead. No. 50016 *Barham* arrives at the rather run down station on 23rd September with the 10.23 Paddington to Paignton. The canopy on the left had once sheltered passengers and parcels awaiting the Radstock trains. (G.Gillham)

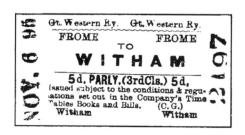

30.   The running lines were singled on 19th August 1970, this applying from Frome North Junction to Blatchbridge Junction at the south end of the cut-off or avoiding line. No. 31259 departs with the 08.08 Bristol Temple Meads to Weymouth on 7th May 1979. Note the temporary support under the roof truss. (T.Heavyside)

31.   Some sidings were retained south of the station and no. 47244 was recorded in West Yard on 10th September 1982 with a special train that provided concrete for the bases of the new colour light signals. Part of East Yard was used by Mobil Oil from 1974 to the early 1990s. (P.G.Barnes)

32.   Two sidings north of the station were purchased by Tarmac in 1982 and the land between them was used for stone storage. The sidings converged near the former West Junction. This is a 1982 view. (P.G.Barnes)

Other pictures of this location can be seen in our *Frome to Bristol* album.

Gt. Western Ry.   Gt.Western Ry
FROME   FROME
          TO
      WEYMOUTH
   4/5 PARLY.(3rd Cls.) 4/5
Issued subject to the conditions and
regulations set out in the Company's
Time Tables Books and Bills   F.N
   Weymouth   Weymouth

33.   Only the up platform has been in use since the track singling on 19th August 1970. The same had applied until 1856, when the line was extended to Yeovil. The Radstock bay had been on the left, beyond the end of the train shed, which is seen in 1995 after extensive renovation. (M.J.Stretton)

34.   Away from the main line, this station is a useful place to stop steam specials for water. No. 6024 *King Edward I* was heading "The Quantock Ranger" from Paddington to Minehead on 3rd March 1997. The roof truss support had gone by that time, following the restoration work. (M.Turvey)

SOUTH OF FROME

35.   Blatchbridge Junction lies at the south end of the Frome avoiding line and the single line to the station can be seen trailing off to the left behind the signal box. On the evening of 29th July 1983 a train of empty stone hoppers is bound for Merehead Quarry, headed by nos. 37241 and 37256. The 28-lever box was used from 2nd January 1933 until 7th October 1984. There was another, called "Woodlands", two miles further west and functional from 1905 to 1953. It had nine levers and controlled a crossover. (G.Gillham)

WITHAM

VIII.   Our route runs from right to left across this 1903 map and the branch to Shepton Mallet is above the turntable, which was in use until about 1936. The station opened before the branch, on 1st September 1856, a single platform being provided. A second platform and a passing loop followed soon after and the line from Frome was doubled in 1875. The first signal box was provided at this time and it was replaced in 1896.

Railway Cottages

Tank

S.P.

S.P.

S.P.

W.M

W

Stati

S.P.

S.B.

S.P.

M.P.

S.P.

S.P.

S.P.

F.P.

○ *Tank*

36.   A down express thunders through as the crew of the branch train look on in May 1948. The nearby village had a population of 350 in 1951 and so did not provide much local traffic. Usually 12 men were employed here in the 1920s and 30s. Back in 1863 there were only five. (J.H.Moss/R.S.Carpenter coll.)

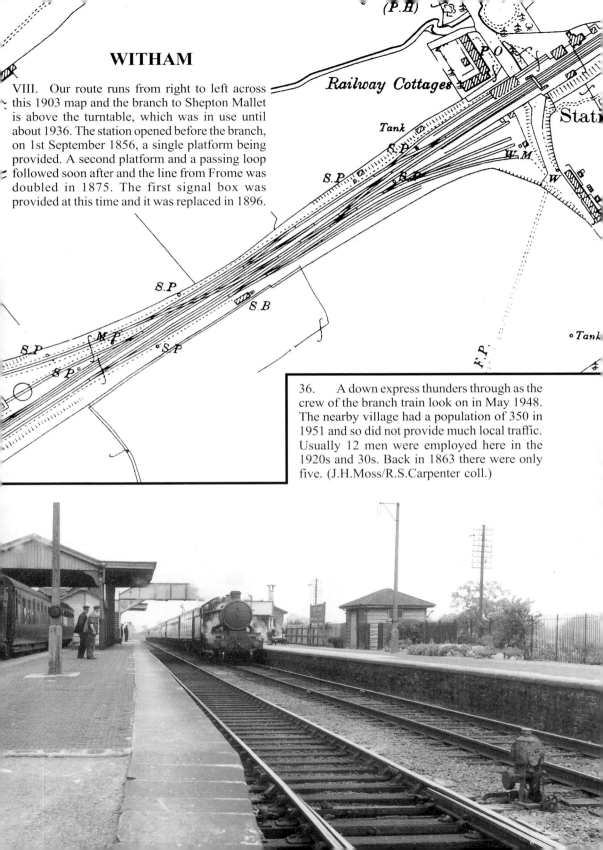

37.   A 1949 photograph includes a small goods shed for passenger train parcels on the right. It was built in 1888. Passengers from down trains could get wet while crossing to the branch train, which stood in the dry in a train shed erected in 1869. The post would carry a pressurised oil lamp at night. (LGRP/NRM)

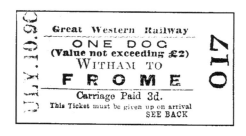

38.   Two more photographs from the late 1940s are included to show the connections to the branch and the sidings. Those on the down side were used for local goods traffic until 3rd December 1963, but the sidings remained in place until 1981. (J.H.Moss/R.S.Carpenter coll.)

39.   An up refuge siding was provided in 1896 and another siding was added in 1901-02. The former, plus the one on the down side, were converted to loops in 1943 to expedite wartime traffic. The sidings had initially served as exchange sidings with the East Somerset Railway. (J.H.Moss/R.S.Carpenter coll.)

40.   The Cheddar Valley line curves away behind the water tank in this 1960s panorama from the footbridge. "3CAR" indicates that DMUs were in use by the time that the photograph was taken from the 1877 footbridge. They were introduced in 1959. (J.H.Moss/R.S.Carpenter coll.)

Other views of this location can be found in the first 13 pictures of our *Branch Line to Cheddar*.

41.   A BR-built 2-6-2T stops with a local train not long before the station closed to passengers on 3rd October 1966. The branch service had been withdrawn on 9th September 1963, but the roof had gone earlier, just one post remaining in this view. (M.J.Stretton coll.)

42. No. 31416 passes the site of the station with the 09.15 Weymouth to Bristol on 23rd March 1979. All mechanical signalling was abolished here when the 67-lever signal box closed on 26th November 1984 and the area came under the control of Westbury Panel. In the right background is the East Somerset line, retained for stone traffic. The two sidings in the distance were also still in use in 2001 for this material. The former bay line (right) was extended to form a reversible loop. (G.Gillham)

43. Renamed East Somerset Junction, the area was the scene of a spectacular accident on 1st December 1987, when most of the 26 loaded ballast wagons travelling from Meldon Quarry (Devon) to Salisbury behind no. 33021 were derailed. No. 59001 *Yeoman Endeavour* creeps past the Old Oak Common breakdown crane on December 7th with stone from Merehead Quarry, bound for Eastleigh. The Cardiff crane is in the distance; clearance took another two days, despite that crane having toppled over once. (S.P.McMullin)

WEST OF WITHAM

44.   No. 6993 *Arthog Hall* hauls a down train past Brewham signal box on 17th September 1957. It had nine levers and was nearly two miles from Witham. It was in use from 1907 to 1966 and controlled an up banking engine siding from 1920 to 1963, during which period it had 14 levers. (E.W.Fry)

STRAP LANE HALT

IX.   The 1946 edition of the 1ins to 1 mile map shows the location of the halt, top right. Cole station, on the Somerset & Dorset line, is lower left. The halt opened on 18th July 1932.

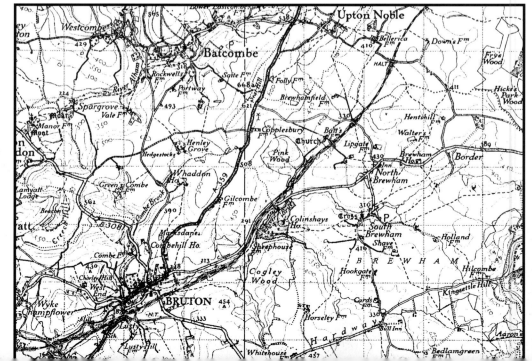

45.   No. 5016 *Montgomery Castle* speeds through with a westbound express in 1934. The signal was worked by Brewham box, which was situated on the down side nearly 200yds beyond the bridge. A catch point is in the background. (LGRP/NRM)

46.   The halt was situated at the summit of the line, the track dropping at 1 in 81 towards Bruton in the distance. This photograph was taken not long before the halt closed on 5th June 1950. It had not been in use between 6th October 1941 and 16th December 1946. (Lens of Sutton)

BRUTON

X.   The 1901 survey includes the down refuge siding (right) that was provided in September 1880 when the line from Witham was doubled. It was lengthened twice. The nearby town is noted for its ancient pack-horse bridge and old established schools. The local population was 2232 in 1861, but only 1700 a century later.

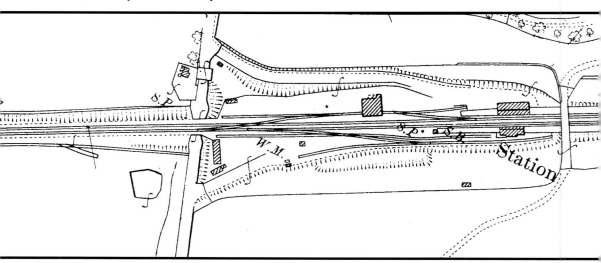

47.   This westward view includes some of the staff, which numbered five in 1863, nine in 1913 and eight throughout the 1930s. The station had two platforms from the outset, but no passing loop. Down trains had to reverse back onto the single line until 1865. (Lens of Sutton)

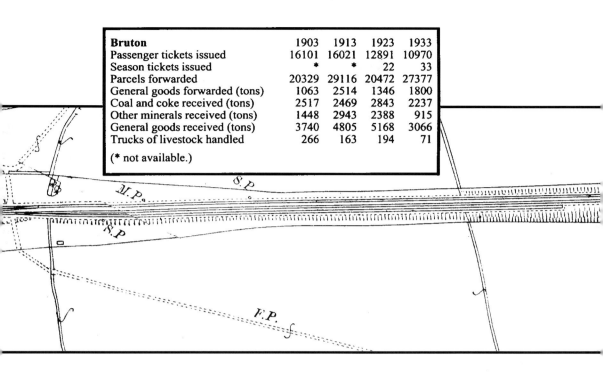

Bruton	1903	1913	1923	1933
Passenger tickets issued	16101	16021	12891	10970
Season tickets issued	*	*	22	33
Parcels forwarded	20329	29116	20472	27377
General goods forwarded (tons)	1063	2514	1346	1800
Coal and coke received (tons)	2517	2469	2843	2237
Other minerals received (tons)	1448	2943	2388	915
General goods received (tons)	3740	4805	5168	3066
Trucks of livestock handled	266	163	194	71

(* not available.)

48.   An eastward view from the footbridge in 1922 includes the down refuge siding, which was removed in December 1963. The crossover lasted until 1983. The stone-built bridge simply linked fields. (LCGB/NRM)

49.   A signal box with about 17 levers was built in about 1877 and the footbridge followed in 1895. This photograph was taken two weeks before the closure of the goods yard on 5th April 1965. A 5-ton crane was listed in 1938. The area was subsequently used for bus storage. (C.L.Caddy)

50.   A new 25-lever frame was fitted in 1909 and the box remained in use until 7th December 1983, but staffing of the station ceased on 6th October 1969. For many years up to 1964, there was a 7.5am from Chippenham that terminated here at 8.19. It returned to Westbury at 8.25. The photo is from 1970. (C.L.Caddy)

51.　Since the withdrawal of main line stopping services in 1962, the station became little more than a halt, served only by Weymouth line trains. Passing the overgrown platforms on 4th June 1980, no. 31230 heads the 06.15 Plymouth to Paddington vans, this being the empty stock of the overnight down newspaper train. The platforms are still at their broad gauge spacings. (G.Gillham)

WEST OF BRUTON

52.　Almost 1½ miles from Bruton, the route passed under the Somerset & Dorset line, which closed on 7th March 1966. No. 6870 (formerly *Bodicote Grange*) is approaching its bridge on 21st August 1965 with the 11.05 Weymouth to Wolverhampton train. Little evidence of the S&D remains here today, although a connecting line was provided between 1862 and 1878. It was never used. (J.H.Day)

CASTLE CARY

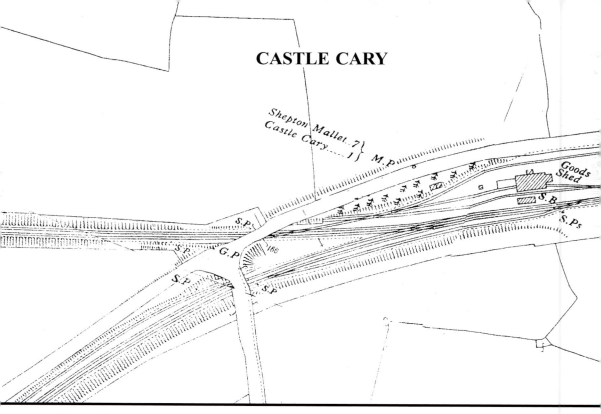

XI. The 1928 edition has our route from right to left and the Weymouth line at the bottom. The road curving across both pages and the bridge over the Weymouth line were built in 1854. The direct road to Evercreech from Castle Cary continued to use a level crossing until 1897, when it was replaced by a footbridge (F.B.) and the road south of the line became a footpath (F.P.).

53. Looking east in 1922, the bridge rail forming the signpost partially obscures the up platform canopy, which was added in 1905 when the station became a junction. The line from Bruton was doubled on 10th September 1880. (LGRP/NRM)

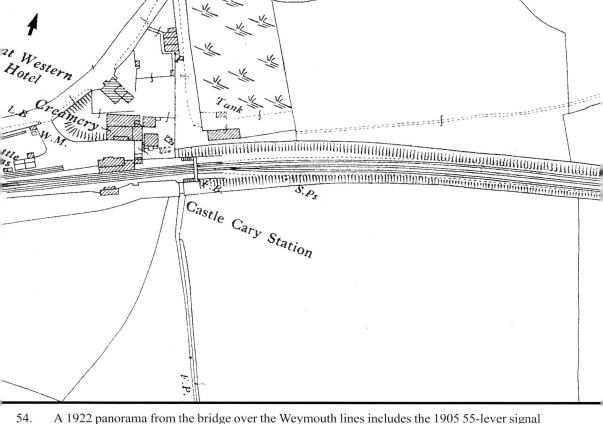

54.   A 1922 panorama from the bridge over the Weymouth lines includes the 1905 55-lever signal box. Its predecessor had only 20 and was built in May 1877. (LGRP/NRM)

→

55.   No. 5745 stands by the parcels shed with an up local freight in the 1950s. There was a staff of about 7 in 1863, 13 in 1913 and 19 in 1936. The yard had a crane of six-ton capacity. (J.H.Moss/R.S.Carpenter)

56.   Prior to the station becoming a junction, the platform spacing was reduced and lengthening was undertaken. The up side building (left in this 1962 photograph) was extended eastwards in 1906 to provide a new waiting room and toilets. On the left is a backing signal. (C.L.Caddy)

→

57.   The white signal box came into use on 27th October 1942, as its predecessor had been bombed on 3rd September. The Weymouth line was singled on 12th May 1968, the goods yard having closed on 3rd October 1966. No. 47401 is hauling the 12.30 Paddington to Paignton on 4th August 1979. The siding on the right had formed a loop until December 1963. (P.G.Barnes)

58.	An inspection saloon is about to be propelled to Westbury by a diesel railcar, having reversed over the crossover on 29th April 1982. The signal box had 85 levers and closed on 3rd February 1985, when Westbury Panel took control of the route as far as Somerton. (T.Heavyside)

59.	An eastward panorama on 18th July 1984 includes the up and down goods loops, which came into use on 28th March 1943. The two sidings on the right were added in February 1941 for wartime traffic. No. 50017 is working the 10.27 Paddington to Penzance. (D.H.Mitchell)

GtWesternRy	GtWesternRy
Castle Cary	Castle Cary
TO
ALFORD (HALT)
THIRD CLASS
5d C Fare 5d C
Alford	Alford
FOR CONDITIONS SEE BACK	W.D

L1744

60.	Some colour light signals were already in place when the 06.15 parcels train from Plymouth to Paddington was recorded at speed on 16th June 1984, behind a Brush class 47. (S.P.Derek)

61.   When mechanical signalling was abolished in February 1985, the opportunity was taken to build a down loop platform for use by Weymouth line trains. The work was well under way on 21st December 1984, as the 08.45 Paddington to Plymouth high speed train passed by. (G.Gillham)

Other views of this station can be seen in pictures 81-86 in our
Branch Lines around Chard and Yeovil.

62.   The goods shed was built in 1954-56 to replace the one destroyed by enemy action in 1942. The nearby siding was retained for use by the engineers, as were two of those seen in picture 59. This westward view is from 28th March 2001. (M.Turvey)

ALFORD HALT

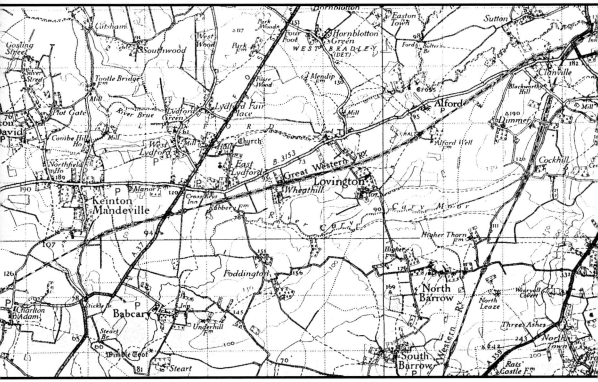

XII.   The halt is right of centre on this 1946 map at 1ins to 1 mile. The junction at Castle Cary is on the right, Keinton Mandeville station is to the right of the A37 and Charlton Mackrell is near the left border. The halt opened on 21st July 1905, before the line became a through route. The population dropped from 125 in 1911 to 84 fifty years later.

63.   This eastward view dates from March 1962 and has Alford signal box in the distance. This was usable from 15th September 1940 until 8th April 1962. There were 16 functional levers and the box was only open when required to give access to an extensive War Department storage area, south of the line. There were 13 sidings in this secure depot. (C.L.Caddy)

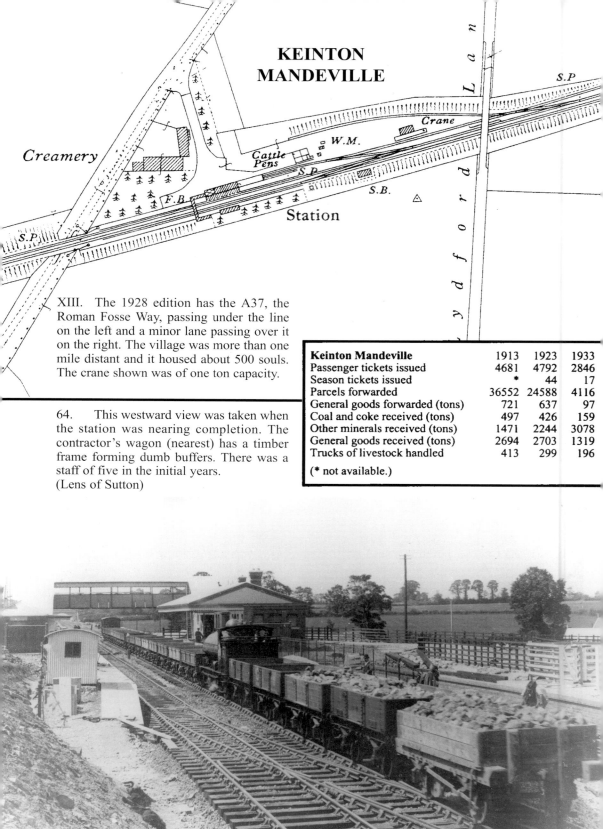

KEINTON MANDEVILLE

Creamery

Cattle Pens

W.M.

Crane

F.B.

Station

S.P.

S.B.

Lan...

Yd ford

XIII.   The 1928 edition has the A37, the Roman Fosse Way, passing under the line on the left and a minor lane passing over it on the right. The village was more than one mile distant and it housed about 500 souls. The crane shown was of one ton capacity.

64.   This westward view was taken when the station was nearing completion. The contractor's wagon (nearest) has a timber frame forming dumb buffers. There was a staff of five in the initial years.
(Lens of Sutton)

Keinton Mandeville	1913	1923	1933
Passenger tickets issued	4681	4792	2846
Season tickets issued	*	44	17
Parcels forwarded	36552	24588	4116
General goods forwarded (tons)	721	637	97
Coal and coke received (tons)	497	426	159
Other minerals received (tons)	1471	2244	3078
General goods received (tons)	2694	2703	1319
Trucks of livestock handled	413	299	196
(* not available.)			

65.   This appears to be an official inspection prior to opening. Traffic commenced on 1st July 1905, both goods and passenger, but only as far as the next station west. (Lens of Sutton)

66.   A 1922 photograph reveals the great length of the bridge at the west end and the location of the signal box, which opened with the line and had 25 levers. Three men sufficed in the 1930s. (LGRP/NRM)

67.   Little had changed by the time of this March 1962 photograph. All local traffic ceased on 10th September 1962, but the signal box remained usable until 22nd September 1964. Train travellers can locate this site by a large collection of scrapped cars. (C.L.Caddy)

CHARLTON MACKRELL

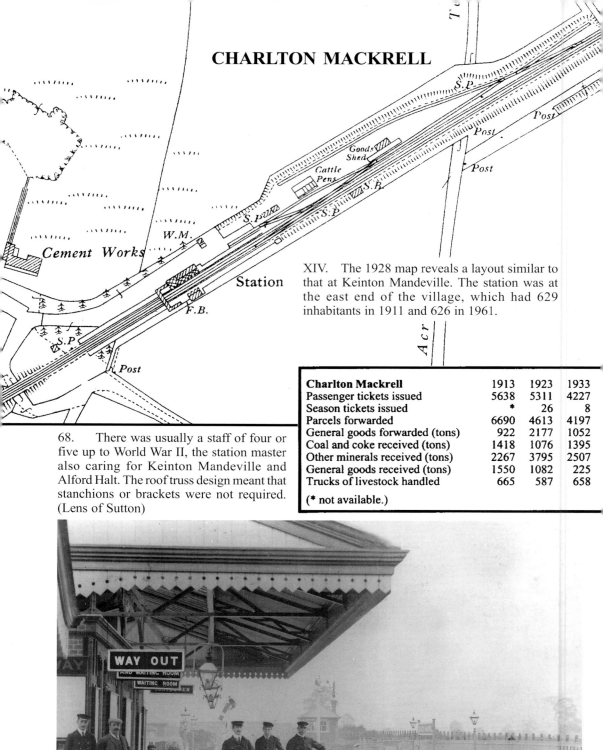

XIV. The 1928 map reveals a layout similar to that at Keinton Mandeville. The station was at the east end of the village, which had 629 inhabitants in 1911 and 626 in 1961.

68. There was usually a staff of four or five up to World War II, the station master also caring for Keinton Mandeville and Alford Halt. The roof truss design meant that stanchions or brackets were not required. (Lens of Sutton)

Charlton Mackrell	1913	1923	1933
Passenger tickets issued	5638	5311	4227
Season tickets issued	*	26	8
Parcels forwarded	6690	4613	4197
General goods forwarded (tons)	922	2177	1052
Coal and coke received (tons)	1418	1076	1395
Other minerals received (tons)	2267	3795	2507
General goods received (tons)	1550	1082	225
Trucks of livestock handled	665	587	658
(* not available.)			

69.   With shift work, there were probably only two men on duty at one time, excluding the station master. The track man on the right would not be included in station statistics. This was a terminus from 1st July 1905 until 2nd July 1906. (Lens of Sutton)

70.   In the absence of a down refuge siding, it appears that a down goods train has been shunted to the up line to enable a down passenger train to pass it. The goods shed, dock and one-ton crane are visible. (Lens of Sutton)

71.   The porter's perspective from the barrow crossing in 1922 includes the signal box, which had 25 levers, six of which were unused. It was later described as "Open as required" and was closed completely on 3rd December 1963. (LGRP/NRM)

72.   Total closure took place on 10th September 1962, six months after this photograph had been taken. Seen in the distance, the first bridge was provided for agricultural purpose and the second for a minor highway. (C.L.Caddy)

EAST OF SOMERTON

73.   Somerton is in the background, as we look south on 28th February 1977 at the 116yd long
Somerton Viaduct. A class 50 is hauling the 13.45 Plymouth to Paddington service over the River
Cary. (T.Heavyside)

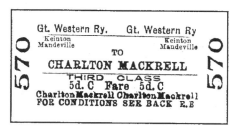

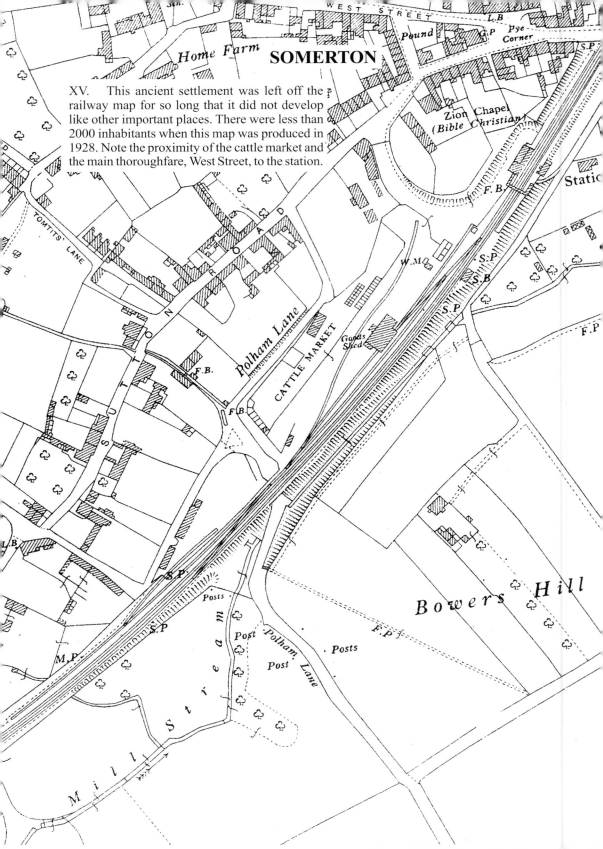

SOMERTON

XV. This ancient settlement was left off the railway map for so long that it did not develop like other important places. There were less than 2000 inhabitants when this map was produced in 1928. Note the proximity of the cattle market and the main thoroughfare, West Street, to the station.

Home Farm

WEST STREET

L.B.

Pound

G.P

Pye Corner

S.P.

Zion Chapel (Bible Christian)

F.B.

Statio

W.M.

S.P.

S.B.

Goods Shed

S.P.

F.P.

CATTLE MARKET

Polham Lane

ROAD

SUTTON

TOMTITS' LANE

F.B.

F.B

L.B.

S.P.

Bowers Hill

S.P.

Posts

Post

Polham Lane

F.P.

M.P.

Post

Posts

Mill Stream

74.   While work was nearing completion, freight traffic from the east began on 20th May 1906, this helping to settle the track prior to seeking approval for passenger operation. This damaged photograph seems to show that only the completion of the platform surface and lighting remained, prior to full opening. (Lens of Sutton)

75.   This photograph was probably taken on 2nd July 1906, when local passenger services started, using such railmotors as no. 15. Through traffic also began that day. There was a staff of seven initially, this increasing to nine in the 1930s. (Lens of Sutton)

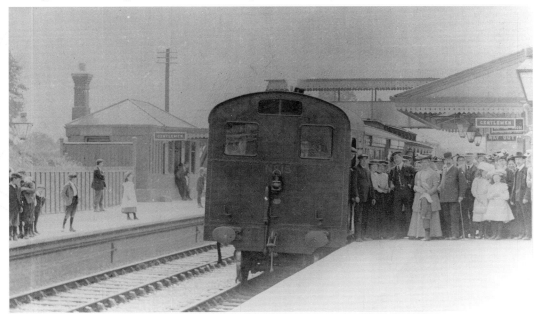

76.   A panorama from the footbridge in 1922 includes a batch of milk churns awaiting an up train, and the West Street bridge. Several houses had to be demolished in this area to accommodate the new railway. (LGRP/NRM)

Somerton	1913	1923	1933
Passenger tickets issued	12207	13106	7210
Season tickets issued	*	82	47
Parcels forwarded	11667	14968	21377
General goods forwarded (tons)	2401	3123	779
Coal and coke received (tons)	1124	833	183
Other minerals received (tons)	1568	1821	1676
General goods received (tons)	2099	2315	3718
Trucks of livestock handled	102	42	30
(* not available.)			

77.   A 1962 view reveals that little had changed in 40 years. The suffix SOM was added to the name, as there is another Somerton in Oxfordshire. Passenger traffic ceased on 10th September 1962 and goods withdrawal was on 6th July 1964. A six-ton crane had been provided. (C.L.Caddy)

78.   This is a June 1969 record of the 1906 signal box, which had 29 levers. A new 44-lever frame was installed in December 1942 in connection with up and down goods loops, which were in use from the Summer of 1943 until December 1960. They were west of the station; part of the up one was retained by the engineers into the 21st century. (C.L.Caddy)

79.   No. 50008 *Thunderer* roars round the curve with the down "Torbay Express" on 6th July 1984. In the background is the signal box, which closed on 2nd February 1985. It had been the last one between Castle Cary and Athelney. On the left is the headshunt of a siding that had been used by Dorset Farmers Ltd. It is lower left on the map. (G.Gillham)

LONG SUTTON AND PITNEY

XVI. Long Sutton was more than one mile to the south and had a population of a little over 700 throughout the life of the station. Pitney was a similar distance to the north. The map is from 1928.

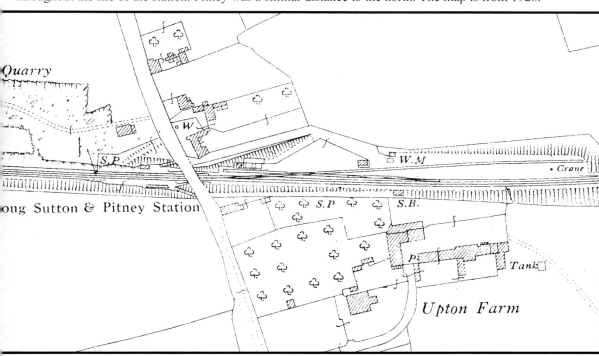

80.   A halt came into use on 1st October 1907 and the goods depot opened on 6th April 1908, when the halt was redesignated a station. It initially had one siding forming a loop, but a longer one and a one-ton crane were added in 1914. There was a staff of two for most of the 1930s. (Lens of Sutton)

81.   The 1914 siding is in the background and the original loop extends beyond the signal box, which was in use from 6th April 1908 until 30th July 1964. It had 21 levers and was reported in 1945 as "open for the passage of the 11.0am Paddington to Penzance and otherwise as required". The frame came from Llandilo Junction. (J.H.Moss/R.S.Carpenter)

Long Sutton and Pitney	1913	1923	1933
Passenger tickets issued	-	5966	3328
Season tickets issued	*	21	9
Parcels forwarded	3561	4985	3559
General goods forwarded (tons)	1395	1120	242
Coal and coke received (tons)	545	182	16
Other minerals received (tons)	776	1584	59
General goods received (tons)	509	632	339
Trucks of livestock handled	336	57	51
(* not available.)			

82.   The platforms were in use until 10th September 1962 and had been extended in 1914. This and the previous picture were taken in the late 1950s. Goods traffic ceased on 6th July 1964. (J.H.Moss/R.S.Carpenter)

83.   Only a fragment of the down platform remained to be photographed on 14th April 1994 as the 08.47 from Penzance screamed past on its way to Paddington. A long welded rail expansion joint is featured. HSTs would not be branded INTERCITY for much longer. (D.H.Mitchell)

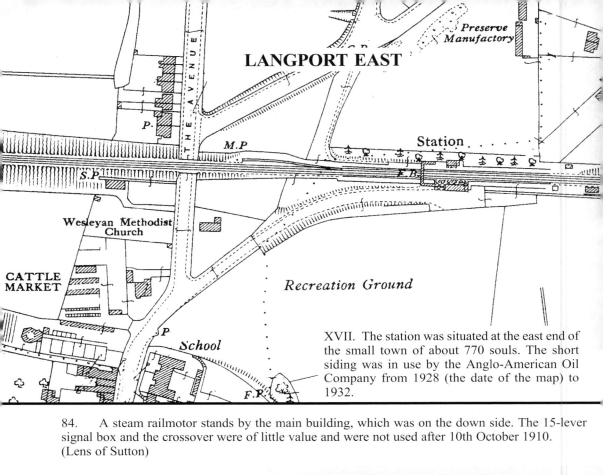

LANGPORT EAST

Preserve Manufactory

Station

THE AVENUE

M.P

F.B

P.

S.P

Wesleyan Methodist Church

CATTLE MARKET

Recreation Ground

P.

School

F.P

XVII. The station was situated at the east end of the small town of about 770 souls. The short siding was in use by the Anglo-American Oil Company from 1928 (the date of the map) to 1932.

84.   A steam railmotor stands by the main building, which was on the down side. The 15-lever signal box and the crossover were of little value and were not used after 10th October 1910. (Lens of Sutton)

85.   A 1922 record from the up platform shows the similarities with the other new stations. Most statistics were merged with Langport West, except tickets issued. These were 11,437 in 1923, reducing to 5513 in 1938. (LGRP/NRM)

86.   The station closed on 10th September 1962, six months after being photographed. Unlike most of the others on the route, this one was gas lit, but like Somerton, its main building stood for over 20 years after closure. (C.L.Caddy)

87.   The up "Torbay Express" is passing over the road bridge on 17th March 1962, hauled by D830 *Majestic*. The town was a long established commercial centre with a good range of shops and a notable maritime history. (C.L.Caddy)

BRITISH RLYS (W)   BRITISH RLYS (W)
Langport East   Langport East
                TO
SOMERTON. (SOM)
           THIRD CLASS
        11d Z Fare 11d Z
Somerton Som.   Somerton Som
FOR CONDITIONS   FOR CONDITIONS
   SEE BACK   SEE BACK T.H

8395   8395

Gt Western Ry   Gt Western Ry
Langport East   Langport East
             TO
CHARLTON MACKRELL
        THIRD CLASS
      11d Actual Fare 11d
Issued subject to the conditions & regulations set
out in the Company's Time Tables Bills & Notices
Charlton Mackrell Charlton Mackrell

8507   8507

WEST OF LANGPORT

88.   After passing over the River Parrett on the 211yd long Langport Viaduct, down trains reached Curry Rivel Junction, where the 1906 route joined the 1853 line from Yeovil Town. "Castle" class no. 5054 *Earl of Ducie* passes with an up express on 6th June 1960. It is the 2.0pm Paignton to Paddington. (J.Cornelius)

89.   Seen on the same day is no. 7036 *Taunton Castle* with the 7.5am Paddington to Penzance express. On the right is the line to Langport West and Yeovil, while on the left is the up siding. On the extreme right is the corresponding down siding. Both these lines were loops and were taken out of use in 1962. The box had a 41-lever frame until 1958 and was closed on 3rd January 1965, the branch having succumbed on 6th July 1964. (J.Cornelius)

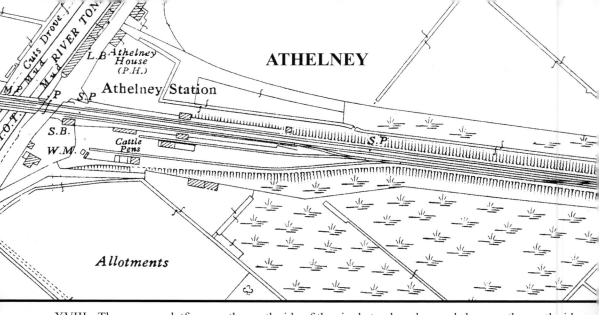

ATHELNEY

XVIII. There was a platform on the north side of the single track and a goods loop on the south side until the route was doubled in 1906. A 14-lever signal box was at the west end of the platform from 1881 until 1906. Two boxes followed, but East Box closed in November 1908, being replaced by a ground frame. This is the 1928 map.

90.   A westward view in December 1963 includes the jibless 30cwt crane and the main building, between the signal box and the waiting room. The left signal is for the down goods loop (in use from 1943 to 1979, but reduced to a siding in 1973); the main line has the centre signal and the right one is for the single line to Durston. There was an up goods loop, with similar operational dates, giving five tracks beyond the gates. (C.L.Caddy)

91.　A closer look at the main building reveals a pressurised oil lamp above the door to the gents. These lamps were normally taken down during daylight hours. Passenger traffic ceased on 15th June 1964, but goods traffic continued until 6th July of that year. There were six to eight men employed here in the 1930s. The tracks westwards were raised onto low embankments in 1906 to reduce risk of flooding. There is still evidence of a "borrow pit" on the north side of the route, near West Lyng. The single line to Durston ran parallel to the double track main line for about ¾ mile. (C.L.Caddy)

Athelney	1903	1913	1923	1933
Passenger tickets issued	8664	8964	10953	8668
Season tickets issued	*	*	47	46
Parcels forwarded	4019	10397	5042	2371
General goods forwarded (tons)	3098	3598	4771	2479
Coal and coke received (tons)	307	264	57	72
Other minerals received (tons)	2316	2512	1271	-
General goods received (tons)	463	788	624	321
Trucks of livestock handled	-	54	31	10
(* not available.)				

92.   The box came into use in 1906 and had 37 levers initially. The two remotest loop points were electrically operated using a hand worked generator. This photo is from May 1970 and includes two gate wheels, the second road (Cuts Drove) being west of the river. This was closed off in 1972. (C.L.Caddy)

93.   The diagram shows only one siding, this being a vestige of the up loop. This remained until a month before the box closed on 5th April 1986. The white levers are all out of use - note the carpet remnant placed over their slots to reduce the draught from the unheated machine room below. (K.Robertson)

94.   The front coach of the 06.26 Penzance to Paddington is passing over the River Tone on 19th March 1986, as the 1972 full lifting barriers were being replaced by automatic half barriers. The crossover in the foreground was in place from 1972 to 1986, after which time the district was controlled from the Exeter Area Signalling Centre at Exeter St. Davids. The box was dismantled in November 1989 and re-erected at Staverton. The South Devon Railway moved the top part of it by crane southwards in November 1992 and it became operational again in October 1996. It controlled the new loop at Staverton from 16th September 1999 and is illustrated in picture 42 in *Branch Line to Ashburton*. (S.P.McMullin)

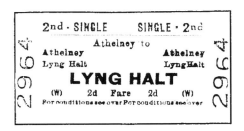

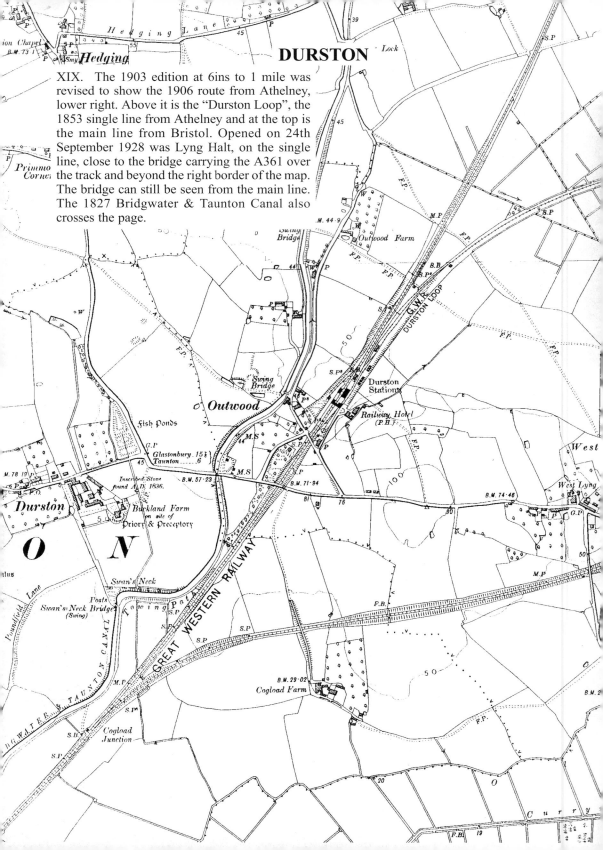

DURSTON

XIX. The 1903 edition at 6ins to 1 mile was revised to show the 1906 route from Athelney, lower right. Above it is the "Durston Loop", the 1853 single line from Athelney and at the top is the main line from Bristol. Opened on 24th September 1928 was Lyng Halt, on the single line, close to the bridge carrying the A361 over the track and beyond the right border of the map. The bridge can still be seen from the main line. The 1827 Bridgwater & Taunton Canal also crosses the page.

95.   A 1934 southward view includes the span (left) that linked the footbridge to the roadway outside The Railway Hotel. Another road descended to the back of the main building, right. (LGRP/NRM)

96.   A northward panorama in around 1960 features the massive 1895 signal box, which contained a 71-lever frame. Most stopping trains from Castle Cary and the Yeovil branch called here, down trains using the platform on the far right. There were only 137 residents in 1961 and thus there was little local traffic. (Lens of Sutton)

97.   The signal arm on the right was for trains taking the single line to Athelney, the single line tablet being collected from the post in the foreground. The goods yard (right) was closed on 6th July 1964 and the passenger station followed on 5th October of that year. (J.H.Day)

Other views of Curry Rivel Junction, Athelney and Durston can be found in our _Branch Lines around Chard and Yeovil_.

Durston	1903	1913	1923	1933
Passenger tickets issued	14588	13918	12384	24490
Season tickets issued	*	*	71	77
Parcels forwarded	6163	8254	14344	4400
General goods forwarded (tons)	1872	2296	1463	635
Coal and coke received (tons)	137	142	183	113
Other minerals received (tons)	2995	3147	4809	39
General goods received (tons)	948	1049	1527	373
Trucks of livestock handled	568	679	236	149
(* not available)				

COGLOAD JUNCTION

98.   The convergence of the routes from Westbury and Bristol caused congestion and so a scheme for quadrupling the track to Taunton and beyond was drawn up. It included a flyover for down trains on the 1842 route. This came into use on 15th November 1931 and is seen on 13th October 1984 carrying a test train hauled by nos 56039 and 56047. (J.H.Day)

99.   The signal box had 23 levers and was photographed on the same day. It was built in 1906 and was moved 484yds south-west in 1931. Its original location is shown on the Durston map, lower left. Closure took place on 7th April 1986. Water troughs were sited west of this location for many years. (J.H.Day)

100.   The massive flyover is in the background as the 15.10 Penzance to Leeds HST runs towards Bristol on 24th July 1982. The Bridgwater & Taunton Canal (foreground) was extensively restored in the 1990s. The junction was named after Cogload Farm, which is marked on the next map. (D.H.Mitchell)

101.   The signal box can be seen above the rear coaches of the 09.12 Birmingham to Paignton relief train, hauled by no. 45135 on 30th July 1983. The outer tracks from here to Taunton East Junction were taken out of use in April 1986, as peak traffic density had diminished and local trains had long gone. (D.H.Mitchell)

CREECH ST. MICHAEL HALT

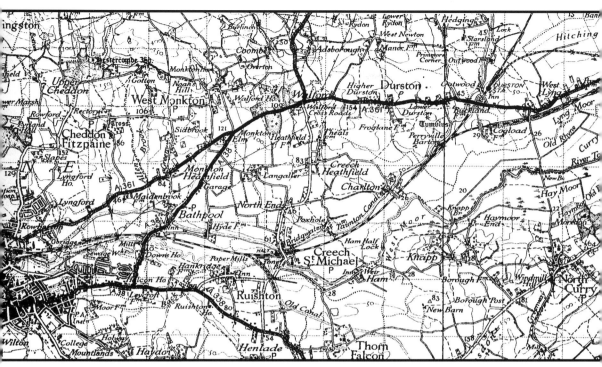

XX.   The halt and the junction with the Chard branch are in the centre of this 1946 map scaled at 1ins to 1 mile.

102.   The halt opened on 13th August 1928, but new platforms had to be provided for the quadrupling in 1931, at which time the population of the parish was 918. The paper mills are in the background of this westward panorama, as is Creech Junction signal box. (Lens of Sutton)

103. Looking east in December 1963, we see the substantial brick-built buildings again, together with the tall posts on which pressurised oil lamps were raised by means of small individual winches. The platforms could only be used by trains running via Durston. (C.L.Caddy)

104. "Western" class no. D1042 *Western Princess* speeds towards Paddington on 11th October 1971 and passes the deserted site. The halt closed on 5th October 1964. The outer relief lines lasted until 1986. (T.Heavyside)

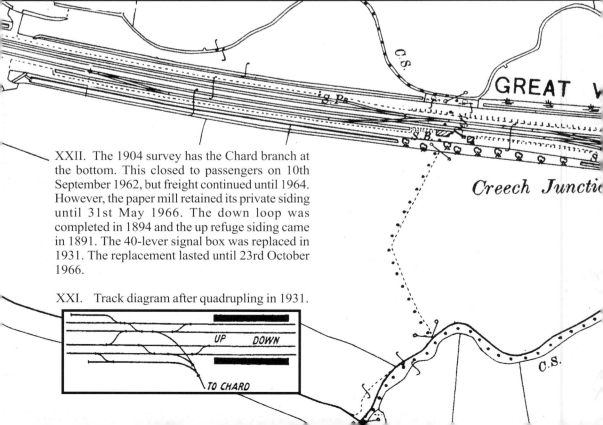

C.S.

GREAT W

Creech Junctic

S.B.

XXII. The 1904 survey has the Chard branch at the bottom. This closed to passengers on 10th September 1962, but freight continued until 1964. However, the paper mill retained its private siding until 31st May 1966. The down loop was completed in 1894 and the up refuge siding came in 1891. The 40-lever signal box was replaced in 1931. The replacement lasted until 23rd October 1966.

XXI. Track diagram after quadrupling in 1931.

UP DOWN

TO CHARD

C.S.

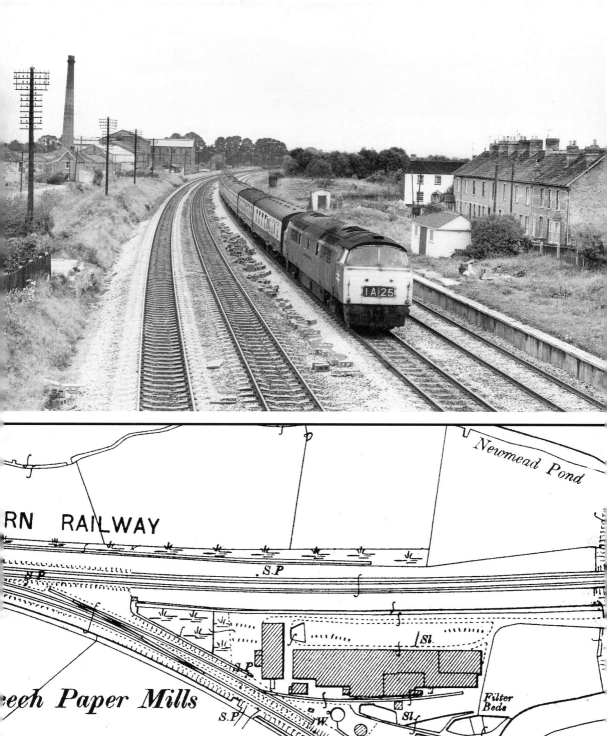

RN RAILWAY

S.P.

S.P.

Newmead Pond

S.P.

St.

S.P.

eeh Paper Mills

S.P.

W.

Gasometer

St.

Filter Beds

Sluice

Five Arch Bridge

C.R.

EAST OF TAUNTON

105.   Having stopped to pick up a Taunton Cider Company wagon, at Norton Fitzwarren, no. 45056 brings the 09.05 St. Blazey - Severn Tunnel Junction Speedlink freight off the goods avoiding line at Taunton East Junction on 12th August 1983. Under the May 1986 remodelling, this connection was removed, and the former goods line was worked as a long siding from the west. (G.Gillham)

106.   With a clear road signalled through Taunton station, class 52 no. D1021 *Western Cavalier* passes East Junction signal box with the down "Cornish Riviera Limited" on 21st April 1976. The two left hand arms on the unusual bi-directional signal in the foreground applied to the up through line. The 1931 box was closed on 23rd March 1987; it had 147 levers. (G.Gillham)

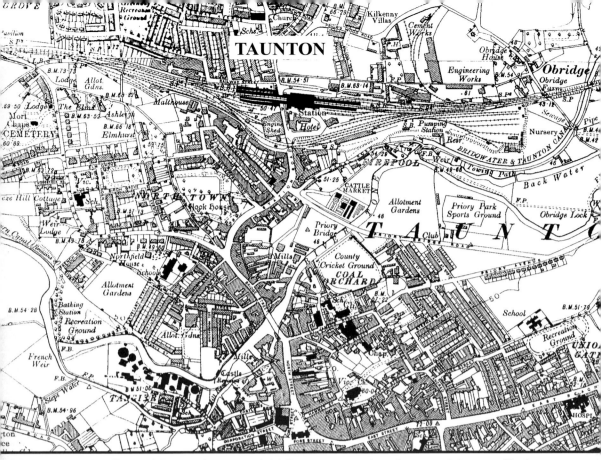

XXIII. As at Reading and Exeter, there were initially separate stations for up and down traffic, but both end to end on the track nearest to the town. These lasted until 1868, when three through lines and two through platforms were provided, all covered in part by a roof, as shown on this 1930 survey. The western section of the Bridgwater & Taunton Canal was abandoned and part of its bed was used for a double track goods avoiding line in 1896. At the top is the "Cement Works". The GWR produced a wide range of concrete components here from about 1899 onwards.

107.   The 1868 main building was built on the south side of the running lines and was recorded in 1913. It still stands today, although the main entrance is on the north side. Most of the bay platforms were added in 1895. The two-storey block is part of the 1842 BER building. (LGRP/NRM)

XXIV. The 1931 quadrupling necessitated four through platforms and extensive alterations. The normal platform usage was thus:

1	Down stopping
2	Chard
3	Barnstaple and Minehead departures
4	Ditto
5	Down fast
6	Up fast
7	Up stopping
8	Barnstaple and Minehead arrivals
9	Bristol stopping and Yeovil

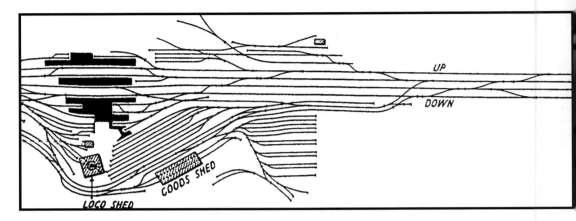

108.   The station was extended northwards, where a new entrance and booking office was provided at the end of the subway. The next picture shows the view inside the doorway. Both views are from about 1931. (British Railways)

109.   Elaborate glazed tiles greeted departing passengers who were only able to buy tickets for up trains here. Another booking office was available in the building seen in picture 107. The Castle Cary autotrain often departed from platform 7, but sometimes no. 2. (British Railways)

110.   Snapped from a passing train on 16th July 1949 is ex-GWR 0-6-0 no. 2267 and no. 5 *Portishead* from the Weston, Clevedon & Portishead Railway. This "Terrier" had been built by the LBSCR in 1877 and became no. 2 on the WCPR in 1925. The curve to the Concrete Works is on the right. (B.W.L.Brooksbank/Initial Photographs)

111.   The running shed is behind the lifting shed in this portrait of two types of 2-6-2Ts on 2nd April 1961. The engine shed closed in October 1964, but diesels were stabled nearby for many years. (P.J.Kelley)

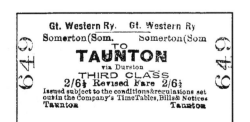

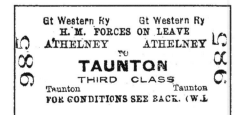

112. Looking west from the island platform on 15th August 1961, we witness a train departing for Plymouth behind no. 7924 *Thornycroft Hall* and rebuilt "Star" no. 4037 *The South Wales Borderers*. The signal box was termed "West Station" and it lasted until 1986. (M.A.N.Johnston)

113. No. 7017 *G.J.Churchward* approaches platform 5 on 8th September 1962, with a down express. On the right is East Loop signal box which had 39 levers and was in use from 1931 to 24th July 1963. East Junction box is in the distance. A siding on the right often accommodated the Castle Cary autotrain between trips. (C.L.Caddy)

114.   A Type 2 North British diesel hydraulic waits at platform 1 during canopy alterations. The pit was for enginemen examining the inside motion, but it would not be required for much longer, as steam was in terminal decline. (Lens of Sutton)

115.   Stepping back a few yards, the locomotive depot comes into view as does a class 08 diesel serving as "West Shunter". It will have moved the coaches from the branch arrival platform (8) to here (3) ready for their departure to Minehead or Barnstaple. (Lens of Sutton)

116.   There was much unproductive shunting and stock stood empty for hours. No. 5185 was recorded at rest on 24th June 1958 at platform 5. The lavatory cistern filling pipes have been stowed untidily - good labour was in short supply by that time. (J.W.T.House/C.L.Caddy)

> **Other photographs of Taunton appear in:**
> *Branch Lines around Chard and Yeovil*
> *Branch Line to Minehead*
> *Exeter and Taunton Tramways*

117.   No. 5563 drifts into platform 1 with a short train from Yeovil on 11th May 1963. More shunting and obstruction of the through lines would be necessary before departure from platform 9. (R.E.Toop)

PASSENGERS MUST
NOT CROSS THE LINE
EXCEPT BY MEANS
OF THE SUBWAY

118.   The island platforms were taken out of use on 6th March 1967, but remained in place. No. 50035 is entering platform 1 on 1st March 1977. East Yard was still busy, coal drops for Western Fuels having been installed in 1964. They were used until 1983. (T.Heavyside)

119.   We can enjoy the same viewpoint in December 1985; at least one colour light signal has arrived. The new road bridge in the background would eventually mark the eastern limit of the quadruple track. Some of the buildings on the left had accommodated the signal engineers. (J.H.Day)

120.   From 1986, the down bay became 1, the down platform 4, the up platform 7 and the up bay 9. Later, the first was not numbered and the others were simply 1, 2 and 3. From 2000, they became 1, 2, 5 and 6 respectively, the latter being used mainly for DMUs for Bristol and is seen here in March 2001. The island platform was reopened as nos. 3 and 4 in 2000. (M.Turvey)

121.   No. 60050 hauls one of the infrequent freight trains on the route, a batch of empty clay tankers destined for Cornwall on 28th March 2001. Note that the two down lines are signalled for reversible working, to improve operating flexibility and thus timekeeping on this important link with the West. (M.Turvey)

Middleton Press

Easebourne Lane, Midhurst, W Sussex. **GU29 9AZ Tel: 01730 813169 Fax: 01730 812601**
If books are not available from your local transport stockist, order direct with cheque,
Visa or Mastercard, post free UK.

BRANCH LINES
Branch Line to Allhallows
Branch Line to Alton
Branch Lines around Ascot
Branch Line to Ashburton
Branch Lines around Bodmin
Branch Line to Bude
Branch Lines around Canterbury
Branch Lines of Chard & Yeovil
Branch Line to Cheddar
Branch Lines around Cromer
Branch Lines to East Grinstead
Branch Lines of East London
Branch Lines to Effingham Junction
Branch Lines around Exmouth
Branch Lines to Falmouth, Helston & St. Ives
Branch Line to Fairford
Branch Lines around Gosport
Branch Line to Hawkhurst
Branch Lines to Horsham
Branch Lines around Huntingdon
Branch Line to Ilfracombe
Branch Line to Kingswear
Branch Line to Lambourn
Branch Lines to Launceston & Princetown
Branch Line to Looe
Branch Line to Lyme Regis
Branch Lines around Midhurst
Branch Line to Minehead
Branch Line to Moretonhampstead
Branch Lines to Newport
Branch Lines to Newquay
Branch Lines around North Woolwich
Branch Line to Padstow
Branch Lines around Plymouth
Branch Lines to Seaton and Sidmouth
Branch Line to Selsey
Branch Lines around Sheerness
Branch Line to Shrewsbury
Branch Line to Swanage *updated*
Branch Line to Tenterden
Branch Lines around Tiverton
Branch Lines to Torrington
Branch Lines to Tunbridge Wells
Branch Line to Upwell
Branch Lines of West London
Branch Lines around Weymouth
Branch Lines around Wimborne
Branch Lines around Wisbech

NARROW GAUGE
Branch Line to Lynton
Branch Lines around Portmadoc 1923-46
Branch Lines around Porthmadog 1954-94
Branch Line to Southwold
Douglas to Port Erin
Kent Narrow Gauge
Northern France Narrow Gauge
Romneyrail
Southern France Narrow Gauge
Sussex Narrow Gauge
Two-Foot Gauge Survivors
Vivarais Narrow Gauge

SOUTH COAST RAILWAYS
Ashford to Dover
Bournemouth to Weymouth
Brighton to Worthing
Eastbourne to Hastings
Hastings to Ashford
Portsmouth to Southampton
Ryde to Ventnor
Southampton to Bournemouth

SOUTHERN MAIN LINES
Basingstoke to Salisbury
Bromley South to Rochester
Crawley to Littlehampton
Dartford to Sittingbourne
East Croydon to Three Bridges
Epsom to Horsham
Exeter to Barnstaple
Exeter to Tavistock
Faversham to Dover
London Bridge to East Croydon
Orpington to Tonbridge
Tonbridge to Hastings
Salisbury to Yeovil
Swanley to Ashford
Tavistock to Plymouth
Three Bridges to Brighton
Victoria to Bromley South
Victoria to East Croydon
Waterloo to Windsor
Waterloo to Woking
Woking to Portsmouth
Woking to Southampton
Yeovil to Exeter

EASTERN MAIN LINES
Ely to Kings Lynn
Fenchurch Street to Barking
Ipswich to Saxmundham
Liverpool Street to Ilford
Saxmundham to Yarmouth

WESTERN MAIN LINES
Ealing to Slough
Exeter to Newton Abbot
Newton Abbot to Plymouth
Newbury to Westbury
Paddington to Ealing
Plymouth to St. Austell
Slough to Newbury
St. Austell to Penzance

COUNTRY RAILWAY ROUTES
Andover to Southampton
Bath Green Park to Bristol
Bath to Evercreech Junction
Bournemouth to Evercreech Jn.
Cheltenham to Andover
Croydon to East Grinstead
Didcot to Winchester
East Kent Light Railway
Fareham to Salisbury

Guildford to Redhill
Reading to Basingstoke
Reading to Guildford
Redhill to Ashford
Salisbury to Westbury
Stratford upon Avon to Cheltenham
Strood to Paddock Wood
Taunton to Barnstaple
Wenford Bridge to Fowey
Westbury to Bath
Woking to Alton
Yeovil to Dorchester

GREAT RAILWAY ERAS
Ashford from Steam to Eurostar
Clapham Junction 50 years of change
Festiniog in the Fifties
Festiniog in the Sixties
Isle of Wight Lines 50 years of change
Railways to Victory 1944-46
Return to Blaenau 1970-82
SECR Centenary album
Talyllyn 50 years of change
Yeovil 50 years of change

LONDON SUBURBAN RAILWAYS
Caterham and Tattenham Corner
Charing Cross to Dartford
Clapham Jn. to Beckenham Jn.
Crystal Palace (HL) & Catford Loop
East London Line
Finsbury Park to Alexandra Palace
Kingston and Hounslow Loops
Lewisham to Dartford
Lines around Wimbledon
London Bridge to Addiscombe
Mitcham Junction Lines
North London Line
South London Line
West Croydon to Epsom
West London Line
Willesden Junction to Richmond
Wimbledon to Beckenham
Wimbledon to Epsom

STEAMING THROUGH
Steaming through Cornwall
Steaming through the Isle of Wight
Steaming through Kent
Steaming through West Hants
Steaming through West Sussex

TRAMWAY CLASSICS
Aldgate & Stepney Tramways
Barnet & Finchley Tramways
Bath Tramways
Brighton's Tramways
Bristol's Tramways
Burton & Ashby Tramways
Camberwell & W.Norwood Tramways
Clapham & Streatham Tramways
Croydon's Tramways

Dover's Tramways
East Ham & West Ham Tramways
Edgware and Willesden Tramways
Eltham & Woolwich Tramways
Embankment & Waterloo Tramways
Enfield & Wood Green Tramways
Exeter & Taunton Tramways
Greenwich & Dartford Tramways
Hammersmith & Hounslow Tramways
Hampstead & Highgate Tramways
Hastings Tramways
Holborn & Finsbury Tramways
Ilford & Barking Tramways
Kingston & Wimbledon Tramways
Lewisham & Catford Tramways
Liverpool Tramways 1. Eastern Routes
Liverpool Tramways 2. Southern Routes
Liverpool Tramways 3. Northern Routes
Maidstone & Chatham Tramways
Margate to Ramsgate
North Kent Tramways
Norwich Tramways
Portsmouth's Tramways
Reading Tramways
Seaton & Eastbourne Tramways
Shepherds Bush & Uxbridge Tramways
Southampton Tramways
Southend-on-sea Tramways
Southwark & Deptford Tramways
Stamford Hill Tramways
Twickenham & Kingston Tramways
Victoria & Lambeth Tramways
Waltham Cross & Edmonton Tramways
Walthamstow & Leyton Tramways
Wandsworth & Battersea Tramways

TROLLEYBUS CLASSICS
Bournemouth Trolleybuses
Croydon Trolleybuses
Derby Trolleybuses
Hastings Trolleybuses
Maidstone Trolleybuses
Portsmouth Trolleybuses
Reading Trolleybuses
Woolwich & Dartford Trolleybuses

WATERWAY ALBUMS
Kent and East Sussex Waterways
London to Portsmouth Waterway
West Sussex Waterways

MILITARY BOOKS
Battle over Portsmouth
Battle over Sussex 1940
Bombers over Sussex 1943-45
Bognor at War
Military Defence of West Sussex
Military Signals from the South Coast
Secret Sussex Resistance
Surrey Home Guard

OTHER RAILWAY BOOKS
Index to all Middleton Press stations
Industrial Railways of the South-East
South Eastern & Chatham Railways
London Chatham & Dover Railway
War on the Line (SR 1939-45)

BIOGRAPHIES
Garraway Father & Son
Mitchell & company